WATCHMAN NEE

A Prayer for Revelation

Living Stream Ministry
Anaheim, CA • www.lsm.org

© 1993 Living Stream Ministry

All rights reserved. No part of this work may be reproduced or transmitted in any form or by any means—graphic, electronic, or mechanical, including photocopying, recording, or information storage and retrieval systems—without written permission from the publisher.

ISBN 978-1-57593-875-2

Living Stream Ministry
2431 W. La Palma Ave., Anaheim, CA 92801
P. O. Box 2121, Anaheim, CA 92814 USA

13 14 15 16 17 / 9 8 7 6 5 4 3 2

A PRAYER FOR REVELATION

Scripture Reading: Eph. 1:3-23

As we begin to know God, His work, and His eternal plan which He purposed in eternity, we begin to realize that the light in the book of Ephesians is abundant, high, and special. We need to realize one thing before the Lord: in the book of Ephesians, God caused Paul to pray two prayers. One prayer is found in chapter one, while the other is found in chapter three. The prayer in chapter one is basic, while the prayer in chapter three is for the building. In chapter one, Paul prayed that we would realize our relationship with the Lord. In chapter three, he wanted us not only to realize our relationship with the Lord, but also our relationship with the church. Now we will speak on Paul's prayer in chapter one.

In verse 17 Paul prayed, "That the God of our Lord Jesus Christ, the Father of glory, may give to you a spirit of wisdom and revelation in the full knowledge of Him." Why did Paul want the believers to have a spirit of wisdom and revelation? He wanted them to have it in order to know the following things:

(1) "The full knowledge of Him" (v. 17). This is to know God Himself.

(2) "The hope of His calling, and what are the riches of the glory of His inheritance in the saints" (v. 18). This refers to God's eternal plan and the accomplishment of His plan. God's calling is for us to be His sons. These sons are His inheritance. God's calling was made before the foundation of the world. In the coming eternity, He will have an inheritance in the saints, an inheritance that is full of the riches of glory. In eternity past God made a decision, and in eternity future God will gain a result. These two things added together make up God's eternal plan and its goal. Paul was trying to make known to us the eternal plan of God.

(3) "The surpassing greatness of His power toward us who believe" (v. 19). This refers to the kind of power God uses today to reach His goal and accomplish His plan. Today this is related particularly to our relationship with Him and His eternal plan. We have to know these few things, and we must receive revelation before the Lord concerning them.

THE FULL KNOWLEDGE OF HIM

Paul asked God to give us a spirit of wisdom and revelation to know these three things. The first is to have "the full knowledge of Him." How wonderful it is that we can have the full knowledge of God.

While Paul was in Athens, he passed by an altar, upon which was inscribed, "TO AN UNKNOWN GOD" (Acts 17:23). In the minds of the Athenians, there was no way to know God. They could not know God by their mind or by their philosophies. They could hypothesize and speculate, but they still did not know God. This is like some men today who say that there is a God with their mouth, but who do not know Him.

Before the Lord Jesus died, He said, "And this is eternal life, that they may know You, the only true God, and Him whom You have sent, Jesus Christ" (John 17:3). He showed us what eternal life is. Eternal life is just the knowledge of God. The Ephesian saints knew God already; we cannot say that they did not know anything about God. They definitely knew God, because they had eternal life already. But Paul prayed in his first prayer that God would "give to you a spirit of wisdom and revelation in the full knowledge of Him."

While the Athenians did not know God at all, this prayer reveals that a Christian, who has received eternal life and who has known God initially, may still not have a sufficient knowledge of God.

Immediately after we believe in the Lord, or a few years after we believe in Him, we cannot say that we do not know something about God. Yet we often depend very much on our mentality or our feeling to support us in our journey. We know a little about God. But other than the little that we know, we very much depend on our thoughts and ideas. If we do not have these thoughts and ideas to support us, we feel that our knowledge of God is not that sure and our reasonings not that sound. Therefore, we often need the support of our mind in maintaining our Christian walk. It seems that when we reach an impasse in our reasoning or in our doctrines, we cannot go on without the help of our mind. At other times, we need feelings, feelings of warmth, feelings of joy, and feelings of exuberance. We need these feelings in addition to our knowledge of God before we can go on.

Yet one day God gives to us a spirit of wisdom and revelation. Then He reveals

Himself to us in a fresh, special, and deepening way, so that we can say that not only do we know Him, but we have a full knowledge of Him. Then we can declare, "Now I know. I have seen, and I am clear. I do not need any other support. I do not need my mind or my feelings to support me anymore. I have the full knowledge of God now."

Perhaps some of you do not understand what I mean. I will illustrate with a few examples. A Christian once said, "I have been a believer for twenty-two years. During the first two years, I tried hard to believe. If you asked me if I was saved, I could tell you definitely that I was; no one could say that I was not saved. I knew that I was saved, and I knew that I had eternal life. But there was one problem: when others asked if I believed in God, I had to push myself very hard to tell them that I did. It seemed as if I was grasping hold of my believing, and that if I did not grasp on to it, I would become a non-Christian. My believing in the Lord was a tiresome believing. Did I believe in God? Yes, I did. But did I know Him? No, I did not. I needed many reasons and doctrines to support my belief. I could only be at peace when I found

5

enough reasons to justify myself and when I found the right doctrines. Only then could I speak to others about my faith. I needed the support of my mind to be a Christian. But today I can testify that I am not like that anymore. I can say that I know my God. I do not need any reasons to support my faith, and I do not need any external evidence to defend my belief."

Brothers and sisters, this is what it is like when we truly know God. This kind of knowledge comes from revelation. It is not a matter of a lucid teaching, but a matter of inward knowledge. This knowledge is unlike the knowledge we had when we first believed, which had to be handled with much care, like a cup full of water, lest it spill. Many people believe in the Lord Jesus in a way that is like holding a cup full of water; they walk very carefully. They are afraid of hearing this or that. But one day God gives them a revelation, and they know Him; they begin to have the full knowledge of Him, and they truly see Him. Then they no longer have any problems. Brothers and sisters, if you truly know Him, the whole world's faith will not help you, and the whole world's unbelief will not shake you. Even if the arguments of others sound reasonable, even if they say that the Bible is false, and even if there are more reasons to disbelieve than to believe, no reason can shake you. You can boldly declare, "I know inwardly. My knowledge is deeper than my mind. My knowledge is deeper than my feelings. Nothing outward can shake this inward knowledge of mine."

This is indeed a very crucial matter. Many Christians live by their feelings. If they feel happy and joyful, they say that God has been gracious to them. If they feel cold and indifferent, and if they lose their taste for everything, they almost say, "Where is God? It is hard to know Him!" Many people are sustained by their feelings. Once their feelings are gone, they waver and shake. They are this way because they do not have the full knowledge of God. God has to lead us to the point that we no longer care if we feel cold or hot, indifferent or excited, because we have known God. Our knowledge is deeper than our joy, our pain, or any feeling. Although outwardly there may be joy, pain, or other kinds of feelings, no feeling will change us, because we know Him inwardly. Brothers and sisters, only this kind of Christian will stand, and only this kind of Christian will not be shaken. God can only use this kind of person.

There was a brother who was told not long after he became a believer that there were mistakes in the Bible. He became so worried that he almost cried. He believed that the Bible was right, and he believed that there could not be anything wrong with it. But others pointed out to him several places which made him a little concerned. He worried about what would happen if the Bible was indeed wrong. He referred this matter to an older sister. He thought that she would definitely be concerned if she heard about some mistakes in the Bible because she loved the Lord and the Bible so much. But to his surprise, after he mentioned it, the sister acted as if nothing had happened. She only said, "It does not matter." The brother thought, "It does not matter to you. But it matters to me." He pressed on for an answer from the sister. Eventually, the sister replied that one's knowledge of God does not depend on such questions being answered. The brother thought, "Perhaps a person as old as you does not need to think about these questions. But I am a young person, and I have a mind that thinks. It is impossible for me to let this matter go so easily." Later that brother spent a year to study the Bible and investigate the allegations. Eventually, he found the evidence to prove that the Bible had no mistake and that it was right. He felt that a big rock was removed from his heart. Actually, had that brother known God, he would not have needed to waste his time worrying. Brothers and sisters, if you have the full knowledge of God, even if more questions come, you will not have any rock in your heart, and nothing will bother you. Others may prove this and that, but Christians can prove one thing—God is God. We know our God. He is so real. Once we know, we know. If we have the full knowledge of Him, every problem will go away. It is not a matter of persuasive reasonings or clear doctrines, but a matter of revelation. Revelation is indispensable. We have to ask God to give us a spirit of revelation, so that we can have the full knowledge of Him. This knowledge is foundational to a believer, and it is quite necessary.

KNOWING GOD'S CALLING AND HIS INHERITANCE

Not only does God want us to know Him;

He wants us to know His calling. He wants us to know what our calling is and what is His inheritance in the saints. In other words, not only does God want us to know Him, but He wants us to know what He is doing from eternity to eternity. He wants us to know His eternal plan and its purpose.

Ephesians speaks of things that span from eternity to eternity. It shows us God's eternal plan. Paul speaks of God's calling, His inheritance in the saints, and His power toward us who believe. This tells us that when a man truly understands God's eternal plan, and when he sees what God is doing from eternity to eternity, he will realize that God's eternal plan is related to everyone who is called. It is also related to the inheritance which God secures in the saints and to the power which He manifests among them. This shows us that God's eternal plan is not something abstract; it is not something unimportant, dispensable, or something that one can shuffle aside. Brothers and sisters, God's eternal plan has a great deal to do with every one of us. When we speak of God's eternal plan, do not think that this is something unfathomable or incomprehensible. No, God's eternal plan has a great deal to do with our calling; it has a great deal to do with God's inheritance, and it has a great deal to do with God's power and its operation in us.

Let us first consider God's calling and His inheritance, and then we will consider the power which is manifested toward us who believe.

First, let us look at God's calling. Verse 18 says, "The eyes of your heart having been enlightened, that you may know what is the hope of His calling." I do not know how many Christians know that there is a hope before them. Many people only hope for heaven. Thank the Lord that there is heaven; it is true that there is heaven. But this is not the goal for which God has called us. This is not the hope of His calling. What then is this calling? Verse 4 says, "Even as He chose us in Him before the foundation of the world to be holy and without blemish before Him in love." This is God's calling. God's calling is that we be like God. On the positive side, it is to be holy, and on the negative side, it is to be without blemish and blameless. Brothers and sisters, what a grand calling this is! If you have never been weak, and if you have never realized that you have erred, you will not realize how special this calling is. But if you know a little about how weak and worthless you are, and how wrong you have been, you will realize the preciousness of this calling. You will say, "Thank the Lord. You have called me to be holy and without blemish; You have called me to be blameless and to be as perfect as You are." Thank the Lord that one day the goal for which God has chosen us will be reached. It does not matter how weak and worthless we are today, and it does not matter how many defects and faults we have today. Thank Him that one day He will bring us to the point where we will stand before Him holy and without blemish as He is. This is what God has chosen us for, and this is what He has called us into. Since He has ordained this, He will surely accomplish it. Now we know the kind of hope we have before God. We have hope, and our hope is to be like God. God has chosen us and called us for this.

Second, let us consider God's inheritance in the saints. Verse 18 says, "The eyes of your heart having been enlightened, that you may know...what are the riches of the glory of His inheritance in the saints." What is the inheritance God has in the saints? The saints are God's inheritance; they are God's possession. This verse does not say that God has given the saints an inheritance. Rather, it says that the saints have become God's inheritance. Paul said that God has an inheritance in the saints. Such an inheritance is glorious. It is not only glorious, but in it are the riches of glory.

In Ephesians 1:5 and 11, the word *predestinate* is used. Verse 5 says, "Predestinating us unto sonship through Jesus Christ to Himself, according to the good pleasure of His will." This tells us that we were predestinated unto sonship. Verse 11 says, "In whom also we were designated as an inheritance, having been predestinated according to the purpose of the One who works all things according to the counsel of His will." This tells us that we were predestinated to become His inheritance. There is a slight difference between verse 5 and verse 11, though the two are related.

God has an eternal plan which spans from eternity to eternity. His plan is to gain many sons. Many people do not realize how great the matter of sonship is. But we have to realize that God's goal is to have sons. God's plan involves sons.

Galatians 4:6 says, "And because you are sons, God has sent forth the Spirit of His Son into our hearts, crying, Abba, Father!" This shows us that God has put the Spirit of His Son in us for the purpose of making us His sons. Hebrews 2:10 says, "For it was fitting for Him, for whom are all things and through whom are all things, in leading many sons into glory." This shows us that when God reaches His goal, many sons will be in glory. God is leading many sons into glory. His purpose is to gain sons. He calls these sons His inheritance. In Ephesians 1, God shows us, on the one hand, that He has predestinated us to be sons (v. 5), and on the other hand, He has predestinated us to be His inheritance (v. 11).

What is God's inheritance? God's inheritance means something that belongs to God. God has predestinated us unto sonship, and He has also predestinated us to be His inheritance. Every one of us belongs to God. Paul prayed that the eyes of our heart would be enlightened to know the riches of the glory of His inheritance in the saints. What is this glory? This glory is to be the same as God is and to glorify God. This is what God desires. He has chosen us to be His people, His inheritance, and His sons. May the Lord open our eyes to see what a glory this is!

Not only should we know Him, we should also know His work, His plan, and His goal. In order to have this knowledge, we need a vision. Without a vision, we will see little; it will be limited and temporary. Concerning spiritual works, we are often burdened with the little projects in our hands. We are happy when we see good results from our works, and we are sad when we do not see good results from our works. Our view is limited to a small sphere, and we do not see the greater things before the Lord's eyes. What we see is indeed trifling. We are like a small child with a ten dollar note in his hand; he is overwhelmed by the note. It is his total possession. Many times, our views are just as small; we do not see the eternal things. We have to realize that God's view is from eternity to eternity. He desires to open our eyes and deliver us from being narrow. Man is too narrow. We are too narrow, and the works in our hands are too narrow. God wants to deliver us from this narrow realm. He wants to show us the hope of His calling and the riches of the glory of His inheritance in the saints. This is not merely a matter of man's need, but a matter of God's need. Why do we have to preach the gospel? We preach the gospel not only because man has a need, but because God has an even greater need. Do not think that the gospel of grace and the gospel of the kingdom are two different gospels. No, they are not two different gospels; they are one gospel from two different angles. On man's side, it is the gospel of grace. On God's side, it is the gospel of the kingdom. God wants to gather many people unto Himself and have many people to fulfill His purpose. For this reason, we should not base our work on man's view only, but on God's view. God wants to gain a people; He wants to gain men to glorify Himself. Our preaching of the gospel and our gaining of men are for the purpose of meeting this need of God. Hence, God's children need a vision, a vision of eternity. A vision will change our work, our view, and our Christian life. Once we see a vision, we can no longer remain in our trifling work. We cannot hold on to our past views and methods, and we cannot be concerned all the time with our trifling gains and losses.

Some brothers and sisters have heard of God's plan and purpose. But when they turn around to work and preach the gospel, they say, "I do not know how to relate my work to God's plan. When I become busy with my work and when my hands are on my work, I lose sight of what I have heard concerning God's eternal plan and purpose. His eternal plan and purpose fade away and disappear. While I was hearing about them, I was very clear. But within a short time I forgot all about them." We have to realize that what we hear can be easily forgotten, but what we see is not easily forgotten. It is easy to forget doctrines, but it is not easy to forget a vision. The question therefore lies in whether or not we have seen something, and whether the eyes of our heart have been opened. If God has opened the eyes of our heart, and if we truly see God's calling, His inheritance, His plan, and His purpose, we will spontaneously see that all our works, both great and small, must be related to God's plan. If they are not linked to His plan, they cannot be considered God's work.

We need God to open our eyes and give us a vision. This will be a great deliverance; it will deliver us from ourselves and from our narrow world. We will feel that as long as the work of eternity is not finished, it is impossible for us to rest. As long as God's eternal plan is not fulfilled, it will be impossible for us to be satisfied. The commitment of our heart, the burden on our shoulder, and the work in our hands will be nothing less than what God wants to do. Even the moving of a little piece of stone should be toward the building of that one work which spans from eternity to eternity. May the Lord grant us grace to remain in this vision. How easy it is for us to lose sight of this vision. How easy it is for our work to come short of this vision. God does not necessarily want us to do great works. Yet whatever work we do must be within that great realm, must be joined to that great goal, and must be a part of that great work. It is hard to say if our life's work consists merely of the little that we are doing. But if this little is what God wants us to do, it is actually a great work because it is surely a part of the work which God is carrying out from eternity to eternity.

KNOWING HIS POWER

Ephesians deals with something that spans from eternity to eternity. On the one side, we see eternity past. In eternity past, God had a predestination, a plan, and a will. On the other side, we see eternity future. In eternity future, God will accomplish His own purpose and gain what He is after. In between the two eternities, within the span of time, what is He doing? What is He doing to accomplish what He determined to do in eternity past and what He will gain in eternity future?

Paul's prayer has two aspects, the subjective aspect and the objective aspect. On the objective side, he prayed that we would have the full knowledge of God and know the hope of His calling and the riches of the glory of His inheritance in the saints. On the subjective side, he prayed that we would know "the surpassing greatness of His power toward us who believe." After we have known God and His work from eternity to eternity, we will see this power within us, and only then will the subjective aspect begin. First we need the objective seeing, and then we need the subjective working. Many Christians have dropped one of these two sides; they have neglected altogether one of these two aspects. They think that they can put aside the knowledge of God and His eternal will, and make it their first priority to acquire power from God *for themselves,* so that they can be more holy, more victorious, and more spiritual *in themselves.* Their attention is on *themselves* and not on God. But God's focus is different: through our knowledge of Him and of His eternal purpose, He will work in us to the extent that we fulfill His eternal purpose. God works within us for the purpose of fulfilling His eternal will. All of our personal victories and individual works are for the fulfillment of God's eternal goal.

Among God's children, many have reversed this order. Their attention is on personal things. They are concerned with their personal victories, their personal holiness, and answers to their personal prayers. This is true of those who do not have a seeking heart for the Lord. But it is also true of those who are seeking, who hope to go on properly before the Lord. Many times, they only desire that their personal problems would be solved before God. Their attention is on their personal problems. Their desire and hope are merely for God to deliver them and release them to live a peaceful and happy life. Many people are centered on themselves. Their lives revolve around themselves, and their attention is only on themselves.

It is true that God needs to work on us, and we need personal victories, holiness, power, strength, freedom, and deliverance. But there is more at issue than this. First, God wants us to see a vision and know the goal of His work, and then He wants to work within us to fulfill that goal. God's goal is not merely to grant us an overcoming life or a holy life. God's goal is not that small. God desires to show us His work which He intends to accomplish from eternity to eternity. Every redeemed person has a part in His plan, and God works according to the operation of the might of His strength for the purpose of fulfilling His eternal plan.

Hence, we must see one crucial principle: the subjective work is based on the objective seeing. The subjective power is based on the objective vision. First there is the vision, and then there is the power. First there is the objective, and then there is the subjective. If a man does not have a vision, he cannot expect God to work within him. Suppose a father asks a son to buy him something, and he gives him some money for that purpose. The father's goal is not to increase the money within his son's pocket. The father's goal is for the son to come back with the purchased goods. In the same way, God has given us power not for our personal spiritual enjoyment only, but for the purpose of reaching His goal. We must deal with this matter in a thorough way before the Lord. We may think that this matter is too broad. This matter is indeed great, but it is very much related to our spiritual future. Many people do not experience God's subjective work within them because they have never received a vision. All subjective work is based on the vision we have received from God. Vision comes first, and then subjective work follows. First we see the vision, and then we have subjective work. First we know the hope of the calling and the riches of the glory of His inheritance in the saints, and then we know the surpassing greatness of His power toward us. May the Lord grant us grace to see that it is not enough for us to be servants in the house of God; it is not enough to merely perform some duties. We must be God's friends, those who understand His heart. We have to see, know, and have a vision; this vision must seize us and capture our heart to the extent that we realize before the Lord that God's work is our work.

One can only become useful before God when he sees a vision; he can only become useful when he knows the work of Christ within him and God's power within him. A vision allows us to see God's plan, while the power enables us to fulfill His plan. The vision causes us to understand God's plan, while the power causes us to carry out His plan. The apostle showed us that we must not only know the hope of God's calling and the riches of the glory of His inheritance in the saints, but we must also know "the surpassing greatness of His power toward us who believe." Not only must we know God, His plan, and His goal, we must also know the might of His strength. If God's power has not done anything in us, it means that we do not truly know God, and we do not truly know His plan and purpose. If we only know God and only know His plan and His purpose, without knowing the surpassing greatness of His power, everything is still objective; it is not subjective. This is why we need to know God. We need to know His plan and purpose, and we need to know the power of His resurrection.

Verse 19 says, "And what is the surpassing greatness of His power toward us who believe." This power is indeed great. It is so great that God must open our eyes before we can see its greatness. It is so great that even the Ephesian saints did not know its magnitude. It is so great that they could not fathom it by themselves; they needed Paul to pray for them, so that God would grant them a spirit of wisdom and revelation and open the eyes of their heart. We cannot say how great this power is. We can only say that it is great; it is greater than what we think and what we know.

Hence, we must never underestimate what is inside this earthen vessel. We have to realize that there is a treasure within this earthen vessel (2 Cor. 4:7). Do we believe this? There is a treasure within this earthen vessel. The treasure within this earthen vessel is so precious that even we ourselves are not clear how precious it is. On the one hand, we see that this earthen vessel is an earthly tabernacle that will pass away. But on the other hand, we see the surpassing greatness of the Lord's power toward us. God's children must know what they received the minute they were regenerated. When a man is regenerated, he receives the Lord. The experience may only last a minute, but it takes thirty to forty years for a man to discover what he received during that one minute. The experience of that one minute passes away quickly, but a man needs thirty to forty years to continually experience the great gift that he received during that one minute, and for God to open his eyes to see such a gift. From that minute on, the surpassing greatness of God's power begins to work in him. Regeneration happens within a very short time. But those whose eyes are opened will agree that what they have is a life of eternity; this life will last for eternity, and there is a surpassing greatness to God's power. No child of God can fully comprehend the greatness of what he received at the moment of his regeneration. But blessed are those who know a little more than others do.

Our growth does not depend on how much power we receive from the Lord, but on how much we see concerning the power we received from the Lord. At the instant we were regenerated, God put such a treasure within the earthen vessel, but we need a whole lifetime to discover the greatness of this treasure. We need a whole lifetime to discover what kind of treasure this is. If a man sees no difference between the treasure he received on the day he was saved and the treasure he has ten or twenty years afterwards, he has not made any progress. Although he has lived ten or twenty years as a Christian, he is the same as a newborn baby. God desires that we see the surpassing greatness of His power toward us through the revelation of the Holy Spirit. Whether we are strong or weak depends on how much we see. Those who see are strong, and those who do not see are weak. The strong ones are not those who have received, and the weak ones are not those who have not received; we have all received. The question today is whether or not we have seen. God works within us not because we ask Him for this or for that. He has given us everything that can be given; everything is within us. Today we need to ask God to give us a spirit of wisdom and revelation so that we can see. Those who see have the experience. In the past, many saints experienced a spiritual breakthrough not by receiving a puff of power from God, but by waking up in themselves and exclaiming, "Thank the Lord, all these things are mine." They did not beg again and again for what they did not have. Rather, they saw that they had everything, and they uttered thanksgiving and praise. Those who have never seen this do not know the surpassing greatness of His power.

How great is this power? Paul said that it is "according to the operation of the might of His strength." We should take note of the words "according to." We have to realize that the power which is toward those who believe is according to the operation of the might of His strength. In other words, the power that operates in the church is as great as the might of strength that operated in Christ. The might of strength which God operates in us is as great as the might of strength which He operated in Christ. There is no difference between the two. I do not know if you have seen this. If you have not seen this, you need to pray. You should not think that you are all right, just because you have read the book of Ephesians a few times and can memorize 1:19 and 20. Whether or not you can memorize them does not count; what counts is the revelation and the seeing. Paul prayed that we might see the surpassing greatness of God's power given to us. If we have not seen that the power in us is the same as the power that is in Christ, we still need to pray for the seeing. If the power that is manifested in us does not match the power that is manifested in Christ, we have to confess that there are still things we have not seen. We have to admit humbly that there are still many things we have not seen, and that God has to show them to us. But whether or not we have seen them, the fact remains: the power that is in those who believe in Christ is as great as the power that is in Christ. Thank the Lord that this is a fact. May the Lord open our eyes so that we would truly see. We do not ask God to transmit more power to us from the outside. We only need to ask God to help us discover and see more of what we have within us. If God opens our eyes and we see, we will praise Him for what we already have.

Now let us consider what this power has done. Paul said, "According to the operation of the might of His strength, which He caused to operate in Christ in raising Him from the dead." This power enabled Christ to be raised from the dead. Every time we consider resurrection, it is a precious thought to us. Resurrection means to be loosed from the pangs of death (Acts 2:24). Death cannot hold Christ. No one who went into death could ever come back alive. There has never been such a person. Everyone died throughout the past ages, went into death, and remained in death; they could not come out. But here was a man who came out of death. This One is our Lord. He said, "I am the resurrection and the life" (John 11:25). He is the life; therefore, those who believe in Him will never die. He is the resurrection; therefore, those who believe in Him, though dead, will be raised up again. Everyone who went into death was imprisoned by death; no one could come out. Only one power was strong enough to enter death and come out of death. That power is the power of God. Brothers and sisters, when you see a man dying and you wish that he could live on, you will realize at that moment how great the power of death is. It is easy for man to enter into death, but it is impossible for him to come out of death. It is possible for man to refuse life, but it is impossible for man to refuse death. Satan's work comes through darkness and through death. But there is a power from God which can pass through death without being imprisoned by death; the authority of the devil cannot overcome it, nor can the power of Hades swallow it. This is resurrection. Resurrection is that which passes through death and which is not affected by death. This power is now within us. The power which raised Christ from the dead enables us to pass through death without being seized by death. This power enabled the Lord Jesus to be raised from the dead; it also enables us to resurrect from death.

This power from God not only raised Christ from the dead, but also seated Him "at His right hand in the heavenlies, far above all." Furthermore, it "subjected all things under His feet and gave Him to be Head over all things to the church." God made Christ the Head over all things to the church. Christ as the Head over all things is for the benefit of the church. This is why the church can receive the supply of power from the Lord. Brothers and sisters, the power within you is such a power. There is such a treasure within you. If you still say that you cannot make it to be a Christian, what more can God give to make you able? You should say to the Lord, "There is no need to give me anything anymore. You have done everything." This power is now installed within you. For a Christian, there is no unsolvable problem, and there is no unsurmountable temptation. The power within a Christian is the resurrection power; it is a power that transcends everything, that puts everything under Christ's feet. It is the same power that operated in Christ.

Paul was very careful in writing the book of Ephesians. He was afraid that we would be misled to think that this subjective work is something personal. Therefore, following the phrase "gave Him to be Head over all things," he added the words "to the church, which is His Body, the fullness of the One who fills all in all." The subjective work is not for individuals, but for the Body. God shows us that His plan for eternity is related to the church and not to individuals. It is the church that is involved with God's eternal plan. In eternity past, it was the church. In eternity future, it will be the church. Today God's work is also the church. Everything has to do with the church, not with individuals. If power is manifested in you today, it is for the church, not for you alone. God wants the church, not individuals, to receive this power. By ourselves, we can never acquire this power. We have to ask God to be gracious to us so that we see the Body of Christ, and see that our life is only preserved in the Body. An isolated member is worthless. For life to be preserved means that the life within is not disrupted, and the life within others is not disrupted. If a blood vessel breaks, and the leakage of blood continues, the whole body will die. On the positive side, when the ears hear, the whole body hears. When the eyes see, the whole body sees. What one member receives is received by all the members. Hence, we have to learn to live in the Body. We have to learn to consider less about ourselves and learn to appreciate the church. We have to learn to go on together with all other children of God. We have to see that the Body is the vessel that preserves life. Paul said, "The church, which is His Body, the fullness of the One who fills all in all." Such a surpassing greatness of power is experienced by those who know the church. If a person does not see the church and does not deny himself, there is no way for the surpassing greatness of power to be manifested in him. Hence, when we speak of God's subjective work in us, the basic unit is the church, not an individual.

May God open our eyes so that we may truly see His work within us. This great power comes from our seeing; it does not come from any other means of grace. The basic issue is the revelation and seeing. It is useless to merely listen to doctrines. If we hear many doctrines, but do not have any revelation, we will not experience any power in us, and the doctrines we have heard will be like delinquent accounts, which can never be cashed or used. May the Lord deliver us from such delinquent doctrines, and may He grant us a spirit of wisdom and revelation so that we can truly see something.

THE NEED FOR REVELATION

We have seen something concerning Paul's prayer for the saints in Ephesians 1. There is one main point to this prayer: he hoped that they would receive a spirit of wisdom and revelation so that their eyes would be opened to see some things. The one thing Ephesians 1 speaks of is that all of God's works are finished. We do not need God to do more works, but we need to have the revelation concerning the works that He has completed. God has planned and purposed. Today God's children need to know His plan and His purpose. "He who comes forward to God must believe that He is" (Heb. 11:6). God is He who is; He never changes. Today we need revelation to see God. The apostle prayed that God would grant us a spirit of wisdom and revelation in the full knowledge of Him who already "is," that we would have a full knowledge of His predetermined plan and have a knowledge of His accomplished works. Many people hope that God will make some new arrangements and do some new works in His plan. But the apostle showed us that God does not need to do this. He wanted us to see clearly that God already "is." It is not a matter of wishing God's plan to be this or that; God has arranged everything already, and we only need to see what He has arranged. We do not need Him to do one thing more; we only need to see what He has already done. Once we see, we will have a fresh experience. We need a spirit of wisdom to understand His work, and we need a spirit of revelation to know what He has done. Then we will become useful persons in God's eyes.

Paul showed us two parts to God's work. The first part was done before the foundation of the world. The second part was done on the cross. One has to do with His eternal plan, which was made before the foundation of the world. The other has to do with our fall and our failure, which were dealt with by Him on the cross. In eternity God had a calling, a selection, and a predestination. Everything He wanted was decided before the foundation of the world. He selected and predestinated, and no one can shake it. From the foundation of the world, man became fallen, and Satan entered in to damage God's work. But thank the Lord that there is the surpassing greatness of His power toward those who believe. There was the fall, but there was also redemption. There was death, but there was also resurrection. God has an eternal plan, and He also has a cross of redemption. It seems as if the eternal plan was damaged by man, but what the fall damaged, resurrection has recovered and brought back. The cross can break the spell of the fall, and resurrection can remove death. We can find God's work completed through the cross and through resurrection.

God's work is completed. None of us need to ask God to do one more thing for us. Some have said, "It would be wonderful if God had made an additional arrangement before the foundation of the world." But Paul said that His arrangement before the foundation of the world was perfect. We may say, "How wonderful it would be if God would do one more thing for us today." But God wants us to realize that everything has been completed on the cross and through resurrection. Today believers do not need to ask God to do anything more. What we need today is God's revelation. Paul did not pray for God to do a little more work. He did not wish God would give us a little richer grace. He did not pray for God to manifest more of His power in us. He prayed that God would give us a spirit of wisdom and revelation in the full knowledge of Him, and that He would enlighten the eyes of our heart to see and know the hope of our calling, the riches of the glory of His inheritance in the saints, and the surpassing greatness of His power toward us. Paul was not praying for us to have more of Him, but for us to see the glory, the riches, and the greatness of the things we have received. What is lacking today is not God's work, but the revelation of His work. What we need today is not more of God's work, but to see more of His work. Paul's prayer in Ephesians 1 is for the saints to see what God has already done. He did not pray for God to give the believers more power; he did not pray for God to do more work. He prayed for wisdom and revelation. This wisdom and revelation will enable us to see what God has accomplished. The answer to this prayer is seeing. This is not a matter of whether or not God has a work. This is a matter of whether or not we have received the revelation. There is a great distinction here. Many Christians are hoping for this and that, as if God has never done any work on them or given them anything. But what is so special about Ephesians 1 is that it shows us that God has done everything; He has left nothing for us to do. God has accomplished everything in eternity past, on the cross, and in resurrection. There remains only one question today: do we see or do we not see? Whether or not God has worked is not the crucial question. Whether or not we have seen God's accomplished work is the crucial question.

Suppose a brother has a terrible temper (using a simple matter as an illustration), and he cannot overcome it once, twice, and three times. He wonders why God does not deal with his temper. It seems as if he puts some of the blame on God. Have you realized that his problem lies in the fact that he still hopes that God would do a work? He thinks that everything would be well if God moved His finger a little. But Ephesians 1:3 says that God "has blessed us with every spiritual blessing in the heavenlies in Christ." "Has blessed" means that it is done. God does not want us to ask Him to do anything more. He wants to open our eyes to see that He has done everything. Hallelujah! God wants us to see that He has done everything already. This is what Ephesians 1 shows us. We may pray, "God, why don't You give me more power so that I can chase away my bad temper and evil habits?" We may pray for greater power, but the Bible says that we do not need greater power; what we need is a spirit of wisdom and revelation in order to see the surpassing greatness of the power within us. If God opens our eyes one day, we will see how great the power within us is. Then we will readily agree that there is nothing greater than this power.

Brothers and sisters, do you realize that the power of resurrection is God's greatest power? The Bible reveals one fact to us: resurrection is the peak of God's work. At the time of resurrection, God's work reached the peak. God wants to open our eyes to see that He does not need to do any more work. God's work in Christ had reached its peak; it is impossible to add anything more to it. As a consequence, in Ephesians 1, Paul did not ask God to do anything more. In his prayer, Paul did not expect God to do anything more. Thank and praise the Lord! God's work is completed. It is impossible to add anything to it. All that God wants to do is to open our eyes and show us a little. As soon as we see the kind of power that exists, it will be manifested in us.

Among God's children, many hope for a future salvation. To them, salvation may come tomorrow or next year. But God wants to show us an accomplished salvation. There is no need to wait for the future. To many, victory is something that belongs to tomorrow or to the future. The aspirations, hopes, and prayers of many people are for the future. But if we have the revelation, we will see God's accomplished facts. Revelation shows us what God has accomplished, not what He will accomplish. Many people hope for deliverance because they have certain weaknesses and failures in themselves. But if God opens our eyes, we will see that our weaknesses and failures were dealt with on the cross. When our eyes are opened, we will say, "God, thank and praise You because You have accomplished everything. Thank and praise You because You have overcome these matters already."

We treasure Ephesians 1 very much because it shows that forgiveness, redemption, and the receiving of the Spirit are all accomplished facts. It shows that everything is ours already, and that we only need one thing—revelation. Once we have revelation, everything will be in place. We are still so weak because we have not seen. We are still so useless because we have not seen. Even though the Lord Jesus was so powerful when He was on earth, we are so weak because we have not seen. The power which God has toward those who believe is the same power which operated in Christ. God has given us this power. The difference lies in the fact that we do not see as much as our Lord saw. Today the difference does not lie in the kind of power that we have or in the degree of power. The difference lies in our seeing. What we lack today is revelation. Once we have revelation, everything will be all right.

This is why we repeatedly emphasize the need for revelation. Without revelation, nothing will prevail. We repeatedly emphasize the fact that it is useless to simply hear something; there must be the seeing. It is a matter of revelation, not a matter of doctrine. It will not do us any good even if we familiarize ourselves with and memorize all of Ephesians 1. But the minute we see, we become a different person. Paul prayed that "God…may give to you a spirit of wisdom and revelation" (v. 17). Other than the Holy Spirit, nothing will avail. Cleverness is worthless, and doctrines are useless. The Holy Spirit alone can open our eyes and grant us sight. When the Holy Spirit truly opens our eyes and gives us sight, we will immediately say, "Thank God that it is done." We should not expect God to give us greater power. We only need to see the greatness of the power God has already given us. A spirit of wisdom will make us understand, and a spirit of revelation will enable us to see. There is the need for wisdom, and there is the need for revelation. We need wisdom before we can understand and become clear, and we need revelation before we can see and comprehend.

Perhaps we have heard of God's eternal plan many times, and perhaps we have heard about the position of the church in His eternal plan. But when do we begin to be related to this eternal plan? Our revelation is the beginning. Revelation enables us to see God's arrangements and His accomplished work in eternity past, and revelation enables us to see what God has done on the cross. Revelation shows us the plan of eternity and the work of the cross, and revelation enables us to understand, see, and know the power that God has toward us. Revelation makes us a part of the church, and revelation henceforth makes us a useful vessel in the hand of the Lord.

Perhaps some of us are very familiar with this word already. But we need to be reminded once again before the Lord of the importance of revelation. We believe that God in heaven today is concerned for His revelation because He has already accomplished all that He wants to accomplish. The question today is how much has man seen. We do not need to ask for anything else. We should be like Paul, who prayed for himself and for the other brothers and sisters that God would grant us a spirit of wisdom and revelation. We have to humble ourselves before God and pray, "Lord, I want to see! I want to see!"